EMMANUEL JOSEPH

The Policy of Well-Being, How Politics, Society, and Psychology Shape Health and Business

Copyright © 2025 by Emmanuel Joseph

All rights reserved. No part of this publication may be reproduced, stored or transmitted in any form or by any means, electronic, mechanical, photocopying, recording, scanning, or otherwise without written permission from the publisher. It is illegal to copy this book, post it to a website, or distribute it by any other means without permission.

First edition

This book was professionally typeset on Reedsy.
Find out more at reedsy.com

Contents

1 Chapter 1: The Intersection of Politics and Health — 1
2 Chapter 2: The Role of Society in Health — 3
3 Chapter 3: Psychological Factors and Health — 5
4 Chapter 4: The Impact of Business on Health — 7
5 Chapter 5: Public Health Policies and Their Impact — 9
6 Chapter 6: The Economics of Health and Well-Being — 11
7 Chapter 7: The Role of Technology in Health and Well-Being — 13
8 Chapter 8: Health Promotion and Disease Prevention — 15
9 Chapter 9: The Psychology of Business — 17
10 Chapter 10: The Role of Government in Health — 19
11 Chapter 11: Health Inequities and Social Justice — 21
12 Chapter 12: The Global Perspective on Health — 23
13 Chapter 13: Health Communication and Advocacy — 25
14 Chapter 14: Mental Health and Well-Being — 27
15 Chapter 15: Environmental Health and Sustainable Development — 29
16 Chapter 16: Health Systems and Policy — 31
17 Chapter 17: The Future of Health and Well-Being — 33

1

Chapter 1: The Intersection of Politics and Health

In today's world, politics and health are more intertwined than ever before. Government policies and decisions play a significant role in shaping the health outcomes of populations. From healthcare access and affordability to public health initiatives, the influence of politics is pervasive. The importance of political leadership and governance in promoting health cannot be understated. Effective leaders prioritize health in their agendas, ensuring that policies are inclusive and equitable, ultimately improving the well-being of their citizens.

The impact of political decisions on health is evident in the disparities observed within and between countries. Policies on healthcare funding, social services, and public health can either bridge or widen the gap in health outcomes. For example, countries with robust healthcare systems and social safety nets tend to have better health indicators compared to those with limited resources. Additionally, political stability and good governance contribute to a conducive environment for health and well-being, while corruption and poor governance often lead to negative health outcomes.

Political ideology also plays a crucial role in shaping health policies. Different political parties and leaders have varying perspectives on healthcare, social services, and public health. Some prioritize universal healthcare and social welfare, while others emphasize individual responsibility and market-driven solutions. These ideological differences influence the type of health policies implemented, which in turn affect the overall health of the population. Understanding the intersection of politics and health is essential for advocating for policies that promote well-being and address health disparities.

In conclusion, the relationship between politics and health is complex and multifaceted. Political decisions and policies have far-reaching implications for the health and well-being of populations. It is crucial for policymakers, health professionals, and the public to recognize the importance of political leadership in promoting health and to advocate for policies that prioritize the well-being of all individuals. By understanding and addressing the political determinants of health, we can work towards creating a healthier and more equitable society.

2

Chapter 2: The Role of Society in Health

Society plays a vital role in shaping the health and well-being of individuals. Social determinants of health, such as education, employment, income, and social support, significantly impact health outcomes. Access to quality education and stable employment opportunities can lead to better health, while socioeconomic disparities can contribute to health inequities. Social support networks, including family, friends, and community organizations, provide emotional and practical assistance, promoting mental and physical well-being.

Cultural norms and values also influence health behaviors and outcomes. Societal attitudes towards health, illness, and healthcare can affect individuals' health-seeking behaviors and adherence to medical recommendations. For example, in some cultures, mental health issues may be stigmatized, leading to underreporting and inadequate treatment. Conversely, societies that prioritize health and well-being may encourage healthier lifestyles and greater utilization of healthcare services.

Social policies and programs play a crucial role in addressing health disparities and promoting well-being. Policies that ensure equitable access to healthcare, education, and social services can help bridge the gap between different socioeconomic groups. Community-based initiatives and programs that focus on health promotion and disease prevention can empower individuals to take control of their health and improve overall health outcomes.

Collaboration between government, non-governmental organizations, and communities is essential in creating a supportive environment for health.

In conclusion, society has a profound impact on health and well-being. Social determinants, cultural norms, and social policies all play a role in shaping health outcomes. By understanding and addressing these factors, we can create a more inclusive and equitable society that promotes the well-being of all its members.

3

Chapter 3: Psychological Factors and Health

Psychological factors, including emotions, thoughts, and behaviors, play a significant role in determining health outcomes. Mental health is an integral part of overall well-being, and psychological well-being can influence physical health. Chronic stress, anxiety, and depression are linked to various health problems, such as cardiovascular disease, weakened immune function, and poor lifestyle choices. Conversely, positive psychological factors, such as resilience, optimism, and a sense of purpose, can promote better health.

The mind-body connection is well-established in scientific research, demonstrating that psychological states can impact physiological processes. For example, stress can trigger the release of hormones like cortisol, which, in high levels, can harm the body over time. On the other hand, positive emotions can boost the immune system and enhance overall health. Understanding the interplay between psychological factors and health is crucial for developing effective interventions to promote well-being.

Psychological interventions, such as cognitive-behavioral therapy (CBT), mindfulness, and stress management techniques, have been shown to improve mental health and, consequently, physical health. These interventions can help individuals cope with stress, manage emotions, and adopt healthier behaviors. Additionally, promoting mental health awareness and reducing stigma associated with mental illness are essential steps in encouraging individuals to seek help and support.

In conclusion, psychological factors play a crucial role in health and well-being. By addressing mental health and promoting positive psychological states, we can improve overall health outcomes. Integrating psychological interventions into healthcare and promoting mental health awareness are essential steps in creating a healthier society.

4

Chapter 4: The Impact of Business on Health

Businesses and corporations have a significant influence on the health and well-being of individuals and communities. Workplace environments, corporate policies, and business practices all play a role in shaping health outcomes. For example, businesses that prioritize employee well-being by offering health benefits, promoting work-life balance, and providing a safe and supportive work environment can contribute to better health outcomes for their employees.

Corporate social responsibility (CSR) initiatives can also impact community health. Businesses that engage in CSR activities, such as supporting local health programs, promoting environmental sustainability, and investing in community development, can positively influence the health and well-being of the communities they serve. Additionally, ethical business practices, such as fair labor practices and responsible marketing, contribute to a healthier and more equitable society.

On the other hand, businesses that prioritize profits over people can have negative health consequences. Poor working conditions, lack of health benefits, and exposure to harmful substances can lead to adverse health outcomes for employees. Additionally, marketing practices that promote unhealthy products, such as junk food and tobacco, can contribute to public health problems. It is essential for businesses to recognize their impact on health and adopt practices that prioritize well-being.

In conclusion, businesses play a crucial role in shaping health outcomes. By prioritizing employee well-being, engaging in corporate social responsibility, and adopting ethical business practices, businesses can contribute to a healthier society. Recognizing the impact of business on health is essential for creating a supportive environment for well-being.

5

Chapter 5: Public Health Policies and Their Impact

Public health policies are crucial for preventing disease, promoting health, and ensuring equitable access to healthcare. These policies encompass a wide range of initiatives, such as vaccination programs, disease surveillance, health education, and environmental health regulations. Effective public health policies can significantly improve population health and reduce health disparities. For example, vaccination programs have eradicated or controlled many infectious diseases, while health education campaigns have raised awareness about healthy behaviors and disease prevention.

The impact of public health policies extends beyond individual health outcomes to the overall well-being of communities. Policies that address social determinants of health, such as housing, education, and employment, can create a supportive environment for health. For instance, policies that ensure access to safe and affordable housing can reduce the risk of infectious diseases and improve mental health. Similarly, education and employment policies that promote economic stability can enhance overall well-being.

The success of public health policies depends on collaboration between various stakeholders, including government agencies, healthcare providers, community organizations, and the public. Engaging communities in the development and implementation of public health policies can ensure that they are culturally appropriate and address the specific needs of different populations. Additionally, monitoring and evaluating the impact of public health policies is essential for identifying areas for improvement and ensuring accountability.

In conclusion, public health policies play a vital role in promoting health and well-being. By addressing a wide range of health determinants and engaging various stakeholders, these policies can create a supportive environment for health. Continuous monitoring and evaluation of public health policies are essential for ensuring their effectiveness and achieving positive health outcomes.

6

Chapter 6: The Economics of Health and Well-Being

The economics of health and well-being is a critical aspect of policymaking. Economic policies and decisions can have significant implications for health outcomes and overall well-being. For example, healthcare financing, taxation, and social welfare policies can determine the accessibility and affordability of healthcare services. Economic stability and growth also contribute to better health outcomes by providing resources for health infrastructure and services.

Healthcare financing is a crucial component of the economics of health. Different countries adopt various models of healthcare financing, such as public funding, private insurance, or a combination of both. The choice of financing model can impact the accessibility and affordability of healthcare services. For instance, countries with universal healthcare systems funded by public taxes tend to have better health outcomes and lower healthcare costs compared to those relying on private insurance.

Economic policies that address social determinants of health can also promote well-being. For example, policies that provide social safety nets, such as unemployment benefits and social security, can reduce economic disparities and improve overall health. Additionally, policies that promote economic stability and growth, such as job creation and economic development programs, can enhance well-being by providing opportunities for employment and income.

In conclusion, the economics of health and well-being is an essential aspect of policymaking. Economic policies and decisions can significantly impact health outcomes and overall well-being. By adopting effective healthcare financing models and addressing social determinants of health, policymakers can create a supportive environment for health and promote economic stability and growth.

7

Chapter 7: The Role of Technology in Health and Well-Being

Technology plays an increasingly important role in health and well-being. Advances in medical technology, digital health, and health information systems have transformed healthcare delivery and improved health outcomes. For example, telemedicine has expanded access to healthcare services, particularly in remote and underserved areas. Digital health tools, such as mobile health apps and wearable devices, have empowered individuals to monitor and manage their health more effectively.

Medical technology, including diagnostic and treatment tools, has revolutionized healthcare. Innovations such as minimally invasive surgical techniques, advanced imaging technologies, and precision medicine have improved the accuracy and effectiveness of medical interventions. These advancements have led to better health outcomes, reduced recovery times, and lower healthcare costs.

Health information systems and data analytics play a crucial role in improving healthcare delivery and public health. Electronic health records (EHRs) have streamlined the management of patient information, enabling healthcare providers to deliver more coordinated and efficient care. Additionally, data analytics can identify trends and patterns in health data, informing public health policies and interventions.

In conclusion, technology has a profound impact on health and well-being. Advances in medical technology, digital health, and health information systems have transformed healthcare delivery and improved health outcomes. By embracing technological innovations and integrating them into healthcare systems, we can create a more efficient, accessible, and effective healthcare environment.

8

Chapter 8: Health Promotion and Disease Prevention

Health promotion and disease prevention are essential components of public health. These strategies aim to improve overall health and well-being by addressing risk factors and promoting healthy behaviors. Health promotion involves educating individuals and communities about healthy lifestyles, such as balanced nutrition, regular physical activity, and avoiding harmful behaviors like smoking and excessive alcohol consumption. By empowering individuals to take control of their health, health promotion initiatives can lead to long-term improvements in health outcomes.

Disease prevention focuses on reducing the incidence and impact of diseases through various interventions. Primary prevention aims to prevent diseases from occurring in the first place, through measures such as vaccination, sanitation, and health education. Secondary prevention involves early detection and intervention to manage diseases before they become severe, through screening programs and early treatment. Tertiary prevention focuses on managing and mitigating the impact of chronic diseases and disabilities, through rehabilitation and supportive care.

Effective health promotion and disease prevention require a multi-faceted approach that involves collaboration between government agencies, healthcare providers, communities, and individuals. Public policies that support health promotion and disease prevention, such as regulations on tobacco and alcohol, access to healthy food, and safe environments for physical activity, are crucial for creating a supportive environment for health. Community-based programs and initiatives that engage individuals and families in health promotion activities can also have a significant impact.

In conclusion, health promotion and disease prevention are essential for improving health outcomes and reducing healthcare costs. By addressing risk factors and promoting healthy behaviors, these strategies can empower individuals to take control of their health and create a supportive environment for well-being. Collaboration between various stakeholders and the implementation of supportive policies are crucial for the success of health promotion and disease prevention initiatives.

9

Chapter 9: The Psychology of Business

The psychology of business explores how psychological factors influence business practices, organizational behavior, and employee well-being. Understanding the psychological aspects of business can help organizations create a positive work environment, enhance employee motivation and productivity, and improve overall organizational performance. Factors such as leadership styles, organizational culture, and employee engagement play a significant role in shaping the psychological climate of a workplace.

Leadership styles can have a profound impact on employee well-being and organizational outcomes. Transformational leaders, who inspire and motivate their employees, tend to foster a positive work environment and promote employee satisfaction and engagement. In contrast, authoritarian leaders, who rely on control and coercion, can create a stressful and demotivating work environment. Understanding the psychological impact of different leadership styles can help organizations adopt effective leadership practices that promote well-being and productivity.

Organizational culture, which encompasses the values, beliefs, and norms of an organization, also influences employee well-being and behavior. A positive organizational culture that prioritizes employee well-being, diversity, and inclusion can enhance job satisfaction, reduce turnover, and improve overall performance. On the other hand, a toxic organizational culture, characterized by high levels of stress, conflict, and discrimination, can lead to negative health outcomes and decreased productivity.

Employee engagement, which refers to the emotional and psychological investment employees have in their work, is another crucial factor in the psychology of business. Engaged employees are more likely to be motivated, productive, and committed to their organization. Strategies such as providing opportunities for professional development, recognizing and rewarding achievements, and fostering a sense of belonging can enhance employee engagement and well-being.

In conclusion, the psychology of business is a critical aspect of organizational success and employee well-being. By understanding and addressing the psychological factors that influence business practices and organizational behavior, organizations can create a positive work environment, enhance employee motivation and productivity, and improve overall performance.

10

Chapter 10: The Role of Government in Health

Government plays a crucial role in promoting health and well-being through its policies, regulations, and programs. Governments are responsible for ensuring equitable access to healthcare, protecting public health, and addressing social determinants of health. Through legislation, funding, and public health initiatives, governments can create a supportive environment for health and improve population health outcomes.

One of the primary responsibilities of government is to ensure access to healthcare services. This can be achieved through various means, such as providing public healthcare services, regulating private healthcare providers, and implementing health insurance schemes. By ensuring that all individuals have access to essential healthcare services, governments can reduce health disparities and improve overall health outcomes.

Governments also play a vital role in protecting public health through regulations and policies. This includes measures such as vaccination programs, disease surveillance, food and water safety regulations, and environmental health initiatives. By implementing and enforcing these regulations, governments can prevent the spread of infectious diseases, reduce exposure to environmental hazards, and promote healthy behaviors.

In addition to healthcare and public health, governments can address social determinants of health through policies and programs that promote education, employment, housing, and social services. By creating a supportive social environment, governments can enhance the well-being of individuals and communities. Collaboration between government agencies, healthcare providers, and community organizations is essential for the success of these initiatives.

In conclusion, the role of government in health is multifaceted and critical for promoting health and well-being. Through policies, regulations, and programs, governments can ensure equitable access to healthcare, protect public health, and address social determinants of health. By creating a supportive environment for health, governments can improve population health outcomes and reduce health disparities.

11

Chapter 11: Health Inequities and Social Justice

Health inequities refer to the unfair and avoidable differences in health outcomes observed between different population groups. These disparities are often driven by social, economic, and environmental factors, such as income, education, occupation, and access to healthcare. Addressing health inequities requires a commitment to social justice, which involves promoting fairness and equity in health policies and practices.

Social justice in health means ensuring that all individuals, regardless of their background or circumstances, have the opportunity to achieve their full health potential. This involves addressing the social determinants of health and implementing policies that promote equity. For example, policies that provide access to quality education, affordable housing, and safe working conditions can help reduce health disparities and promote well-being.

Community engagement and empowerment are also essential components of addressing health inequities. By involving communities in the development and implementation of health policies and programs, we can ensure that they are culturally appropriate and address the specific needs of different populations. Empowering individuals and communities to take control of their health can lead to more sustainable and effective health outcomes.

In conclusion, addressing health inequities requires a commitment to social justice and a comprehensive approach that involves addressing social determinants of health, implementing equitable policies, and engaging and empowering communities. By promoting fairness and equity in health, we can create a more just and inclusive society that supports the well-being of all individuals.

12

Chapter 12: The Global Perspective on Health

Health is a global issue that transcends national borders. Global health involves the study and practice of improving health and achieving equity in health for all people worldwide. This field encompasses a wide range of issues, including infectious diseases, non-communicable diseases, maternal and child health, and health systems strengthening. Addressing global health challenges requires international collaboration and cooperation.

Infectious diseases, such as HIV/AIDS, tuberculosis, and malaria, continue to pose significant challenges to global health. Efforts to combat these diseases involve prevention, treatment, and research initiatives that require collaboration between countries, international organizations, and non-governmental organizations. Global health organizations, such as the World Health Organization (WHO) and the Global Fund, play a crucial role in coordinating and supporting these efforts.

Non-communicable diseases (NCDs), such as heart disease, diabetes, and cancer, are also a growing concern in global health. The rise in NCDs is often linked to lifestyle factors, such as poor diet, physical inactivity, and tobacco use. Addressing the global burden of NCDs requires a multi-faceted approach that includes prevention, early detection, and effective management.

International cooperation and the sharing of best practices can help countries develop and implement effective strategies to combat NCDs.

In conclusion, global health is a complex and multi-dimensional field that requires international collaboration and cooperation. By addressing infectious diseases, non-communicable diseases, and other global health challenges, we can work towards achieving health equity and improving health outcomes for all people worldwide.

13

Chapter 13: Health Communication and Advocacy

Effective health communication and advocacy are essential for promoting health and well-being. Health communication involves the exchange of information to influence health behaviors and improve health outcomes. This includes health education campaigns, public health messaging, and health literacy initiatives. By providing accurate and accessible information, health communication can empower individuals to make informed decisions about their health.

Health advocacy involves the promotion of policies and practices that support health and well-being. Advocates work to influence public opinion, policy decisions, and resource allocation to address health issues and promote health equity. This can involve lobbying for legislation, raising awareness about health issues, and mobilizing communities to take action. Effective health advocacy requires collaboration between individuals, communities, and organizations.

The use of media and technology has transformed health communication and advocacy. Social media platforms, websites, and mobile apps provide new opportunities for reaching and engaging with diverse audiences. These tools can be used to disseminate health information, promote health behaviors, and advocate for policy changes. However, it is essential to ensure that the information shared is accurate and evidence-based to avoid misinformation and promote public trust.

In conclusion, effective health communication and advocacy are crucial for promoting health and well-being. By providing accurate information and advocating for policies that support health, we can empower individuals and communities to make informed decisions and take action to improve their health. The use of media and technology can enhance these efforts and reach a broader audience.

14

Chapter 14: Mental Health and Well-Being

Mental health is a critical component of overall well-being. It encompasses emotional, psychological, and social well-being and affects how individuals think, feel, and behave. Mental health influences various aspects of life, including relationships, work, and physical health. Addressing mental health requires a comprehensive approach that includes prevention, early intervention, and access to mental health services.

Prevention involves addressing risk factors and promoting protective factors that influence mental health. This can include initiatives that promote healthy lifestyles, build resilience, and reduce stress. Early intervention involves identifying and addressing mental health issues before they become severe. This can involve screening programs, mental health education, and providing support for individuals at risk of developing mental health conditions.

Access to mental health services is crucial for addressing mental health issues and promoting well-being. This includes providing affordable and accessible mental health care, reducing stigma associated with mental illness, and integrating mental health services into primary care. Collaboration between healthcare providers, communities, and policymakers is essential for ensuring that individuals have access to the mental health care they need.

In conclusion, mental health is a vital aspect of overall well-being. By addressing risk factors, promoting early intervention, and ensuring access to mental health services, we can improve mental health outcomes and enhance overall well-being. A comprehensive and collaborative approach is essential for promoting mental health and addressing the mental health needs of individuals and communities.

15

Chapter 15: Environmental Health and Sustainable Development

Environmental health is a critical aspect of overall well-being, as the environment significantly influences health outcomes. Factors such as air and water quality, exposure to hazardous substances, and access to green spaces can impact physical and mental health. Addressing environmental health requires a comprehensive approach that includes monitoring, regulation, and community engagement.

Air and water quality are essential components of environmental health. Poor air quality, resulting from pollution and emissions, can lead to respiratory diseases, cardiovascular problems, and other health issues. Ensuring clean and safe drinking water is crucial for preventing waterborne diseases and promoting overall health. Policies and regulations that limit pollution, protect natural resources, and promote sustainable practices are essential for maintaining a healthy environment.

Exposure to hazardous substances, such as chemicals, pesticides, and heavy metals, can have detrimental effects on health. Effective regulation and monitoring of these substances are crucial for preventing adverse health outcomes. Additionally, public education and awareness campaigns can help individuals reduce their exposure to harmful substances and adopt safer practices.

Access to green spaces and natural environments is also important for mental and physical well-being. Green spaces provide opportunities for physical activity, relaxation, and social interaction, contributing to improved mental health and reduced stress. Urban planning and development that prioritize green spaces and sustainable practices can enhance the quality of life for communities.

In conclusion, environmental health is a vital component of overall well-being. Addressing environmental health requires a comprehensive approach that includes monitoring, regulation, and community engagement. By promoting clean air and water, reducing exposure to hazardous substances, and ensuring access to green spaces, we can create a healthier and more sustainable environment for all.

16

Chapter 16: Health Systems and Policy

Health systems play a crucial role in delivering healthcare services and promoting well-being. A well-functioning health system ensures that individuals have access to quality healthcare, regardless of their socioeconomic status. Health systems encompass a range of components, including healthcare providers, facilities, financing mechanisms, and governance structures. Effective health systems require adequate resources, skilled healthcare workers, and efficient management.

One of the key components of a health system is healthcare financing. Adequate funding is essential for ensuring that healthcare services are accessible and affordable. Different countries adopt various healthcare financing models, such as public funding, private insurance, or a combination of both. Universal healthcare systems, funded by public taxes, aim to provide equitable access to healthcare services for all individuals. In contrast, private insurance models may result in disparities in access and affordability.

Health workforce is another critical component of health systems. Skilled healthcare workers, including doctors, nurses, and allied health professionals, are essential for delivering quality healthcare services. Ensuring that healthcare workers are adequately trained, supported, and motivated is crucial for the effectiveness of health systems. Additionally, addressing workforce shortages and maldistribution, particularly in rural and underserved areas, is essential for equitable healthcare delivery.

Governance and management are also vital for the functioning of health systems. Effective governance involves setting policies, regulations, and standards for healthcare delivery, as well as ensuring accountability and transparency. Efficient management ensures that resources are used effectively and services are delivered in a timely and coordinated manner. Collaboration between government, healthcare providers, and communities is essential for the success of health systems.

In conclusion, health systems play a critical role in delivering healthcare services and promoting well-being. Adequate financing, skilled healthcare workers, and effective governance and management are essential components of well-functioning health systems. By ensuring that health systems are adequately resourced and efficiently managed, we can create a supportive environment for health and improve health outcomes for all individuals.

17

Chapter 17: The Future of Health and Well-Being

As we look towards the future, the landscape of health and well-being is constantly evolving. Advances in technology, changes in societal values, and shifts in political and economic landscapes will all play a role in shaping the future of health. Embracing these changes and anticipating future challenges and opportunities will be essential for promoting health and well-being.

Technological advancements, such as artificial intelligence, genomics, and telehealth, have the potential to revolutionize healthcare delivery and improve health outcomes. These innovations can enhance diagnostic accuracy, personalize treatments, and expand access to healthcare services. However, it is crucial to ensure that these technologies are used ethically and equitably, to avoid exacerbating existing health disparities.

Societal values and cultural norms will also influence the future of health and well-being. As societies become more diverse and interconnected, there will be a greater emphasis on inclusivity and equity in health policies and practices. Recognizing and addressing the unique health needs of different populations, including marginalized and vulnerable groups, will be essential for promoting health equity.

Political and economic factors will continue to shape the future of health.

Policy decisions, healthcare financing, and economic stability will all impact the accessibility and affordability of healthcare services. It is essential for governments, organizations, and communities to work together to create a supportive environment for health. This includes implementing policies that address social determinants of health, ensuring equitable access to healthcare, and promoting economic stability.

In conclusion, the future of health and well-being will be shaped by technological advancements, societal values, and political and economic factors. Embracing these changes and anticipating future challenges and opportunities will be essential for promoting health and well-being. By working together and adopting a comprehensive and equitable approach, we can create a healthier and more inclusive future for all.

The Policy of Well-Being: How Politics, Society, and Psychology Shape Health and Business

Description:

In "The Policy of Well-Being," explore the fascinating intersection of politics, society, and psychology, and how they collectively influence health and business. This comprehensive book delves into the critical factors that shape our well-being, from government policies and societal values to psychological states and corporate practices.

Through 17 insightful chapters, the book examines the role of political decisions in healthcare access and public health initiatives, the impact of social determinants on health disparities, and the profound connection between mental health and overall well-being. It also highlights the influence of business practices on employee health and community well-being, the importance of public health policies, and the economics of health and well-being.

With a focus on global health, environmental health, and health systems, the book addresses pressing challenges and offers solutions for creating a healthier and more equitable future. It emphasizes the significance of effective health communication, advocacy, and mental health support, and explores the potential of technological advancements in transforming healthcare.

"The Policy of Well-Being" is an essential read for policymakers, health

CHAPTER 17: THE FUTURE OF HEALTH AND WELL-BEING

professionals, business leaders, and anyone interested in understanding the complex factors that shape our health and well-being. By adopting a holistic and interdisciplinary approach, the book provides valuable insights and practical strategies for promoting health equity and enhancing overall well-being.

www.ingramcontent.com/pod-product-compliance
Lightning Source LLC
LaVergne TN
LVHW020739090526
838202LV00057BA/6046